Overcoming the Odds

Dan O'Brien

Bill Gutman

RSVP

RAINTREE
STECK-VAUGHN
P U B L I S H E R S
The Steck-Vaughn Company

Austin, Texas

Published by Raintree Steck-Vaughn Publishers,
an imprint of Steck-Vaughn Company

Developed for Steck-Vaughn Company by
Visual Education Corporation, Princeton, New Jersey
Editor: Marilyn Miller
Photo Research: Marty Levick
Electronic Preparation: Cynthia C. Feldner, *Manager;* Elaine Weiss
Production Supervisor: Ellen Foos
Electronic Production: Lisa Evans-Skopas, *Manager;* Elise Dodeles, Deirdre Sheean
Interior Design: Maxson Crandall

Raintree Steck-Vaughn Publishers staff
Editor: Kathy DeVico
Project Manager: Joyce Spicer

Photo Credits: Cover: © Mike Powell/ALLSPORT; 4: © Jerry Lampen/REUTERS/Archive Photos;
6: © Tom Szlukovenyi/REUTERS/Archive Photos; 7: © Wolfgang Rattay/REUTERS/Archive Photos;
10: © 1993 Henley High School Yearbook; 12: © Doug Mills/AP/Wide World Photos, Inc.;
21: © Leita Cowart/AP/Wide World Photos, Inc.; 24: © Mike Powell/ALLSPORT;
26: © 1992 Steven E. Sutton/Duomo; 27: © Tim Defrisco/ALLSPORT; 28: © Mike Powell/ALLSPORT;
29: © Gary Hershorn/REUTERS/Archive Photos; 32: © Richard Martin/Vandystadt/ALLSPORT;
34: © Richard Martin/Vandystadt/ALLSPORT; 39: © Paul Sakuma/AP/Wide World Photos, Inc.;
40: © Tom Szlukovenyi/REUTERS/Archive Photos; 41: © Mike Powell/ALLSPORT;
42: © Tannen Maury/AP/Wide World Photos, Inc.; 43: © HO/AP/Wide World Photos, Inc.

Library of Congress Cataloging-in-Publication Data
Gutman, Bill.
    Dan O'Brien / Bill Gutman.
        p.   cm. — (Overcoming the odds)
    Includes bibliographical references (p. 46) and index.
    Summary: Describes the training, competitions, and triumph over an attention
deficit disorder of the winner of the decathlon in the 1996 Olympic games.
    ISBN 0-8172-4129-9
    1. O'Brien, Dan, 1966– —Juvenile literature.   2. Track and field athletes—
United States—Biography—Juvenile literature.   3. Decathlon—Juvenile literature.
[1. O'Brien, Dan, 1966–.   2. Track and field athletes.   3. Decathlon.]   I. Title.
II. Series.
GV697.027G88 1998
796.4′2′092—dc21
[B]   97–15791
                                                                                              CIP
                                                                                               AC

Printed and bound in the United States
1 2 3 4 5 6 7 8 9 0   WZ   01 00 99 98 97

Table of Contents

Chapter 1

The Quest for Olympic Gold

A crowd of 80,000 people packed Olympic Stadium in Atlanta, Georgia, on the night of August 1, 1996. The fans were there to watch track-and-field events in the 26th (XXVI) Summer Olympic Games. The Atlanta games were nicknamed the Centennial Olympics, because the first modern Olympic Games were held in Athens, Greece, 100 years earlier, in 1896.

Just 13 countries and 311 athletes took part in those first games. But in Atlanta, a record 197 countries and an estimated 11,000 athletes participated. Of all the athletes competing, perhaps none wanted to win a gold medal more than Dan O'Brien of the United States. Dan was the favorite in one of the most difficult events in the Olympics—the decathlon.

The decathlon—which consists of ten different track-and-field events and involves running, jumping, throwing, and vaulting—takes great skill and endurance. The events are held over two days, with five events each day. Points are awarded for times and distances in each event. At the end, the athlete

Dan holds the American flag on his shoulders after winning the gold medal in the men's decathlon at the 1996 Olympics.

with the most points wins. Now, on the night of August 1, the competitors lined up for the tenth and final event—the 1,500-meter run.

After nine events, Dan O'Brien was in first place. He led Germany's Frank Busemann by 209 points. All Dan had to do to win the gold medal was finish the 1,500-meter run less than 32 seconds behind Busemann.

When the starter's gun sounded, Busemann took off quickly. He knew that he would have to push hard to beat O'Brien by 32 seconds or more. Dan looked sluggish, jogging at a seemingly slow pace. He quickly fell behind not only Busemann but also a number of the other runners.

Then Dan began to pick up the pace, closing the gap on Busemann. The crowd was screaming as Dan kept within a safe distance of the German decathlete.

"The Olympics and the medal," Dan said about the games. "That just kept ringing in my head. I just wouldn't be satisfied with anything else. It was a win-lose situation. I didn't see any real in-between."

Dan celebrates his victory in the men's decathlon in the 1996 Olympics in Atlanta.

Dan stands between silver medalist Frank Busemann, on his left, and bronze medalist Tomas Dvorak, on his right, during the medal ceremony at the 1996 Olympics.

That's because Dan knew what a long, hard road it had been for him. He'd had to overcome many obstacles along the way. Dan finally became the best in the world in 1991 and was expected to win the gold medal at the 1992 Olympics in Barcelona, Spain. But he failed to make the team after one disastrous event in the Olympic Trials.

For four long years, Dan had to live with that failure. Now, as he came into the final lap of the 1,500, he saw that he was about to realize his lifelong dream. Sensing his victory, the 80,000 fans in Olympic Stadium began to cheer even louder.

"The crowd made the difference," Dan said later. "I was coming off the third lap, and I heard only 'U–S–A,' 'U–S–A,' 'U–S–A,' in my head. It drove me to the finish."

Dan crossed the finish line 14.48 seconds behind Busemann. This time was good enough to give him his Olympic gold medal—at last!

Chapter 2

An Athlete Emerges

For the first two years of his life, Dan O'Brien didn't have a stable home. He was born on July 18, 1966, in Portland, Oregon. His father was African American, and his mother was white and came from Finland. Both were college students, and they decided that they weren't in a good position to raise a baby. So they put Dan up for adoption as soon as he was born.

It isn't always easy to find a family for a baby of mixed race. It took two years, while he lived in foster homes, before Dan was adopted by Jim and Virginia O'Brien of Klamath Falls, Oregon. The O'Briens were a rare couple who opened their hearts to children who needed a home and a family.

The O'Briens had two children of their own. After Dan, they adopted five more children. All eight children grew up in a nine-bedroom converted barn, and they traveled as a family in an old school bus they named Gulliver. Dan grew up in a multiethnic household, which included brothers and sisters of Korean, Mexican, and Native American heritage.

Jim O'Brien remembers that even at the age of two, Dan showed signs of athletic ability. As Mr. O'Brien put it, when other kids his age were just "waddling," Dan was already jumping off tables and running.

During his early years, Dan wasn't a good student. He had a natural intelligence, yet he never seemed to do as well as he should in school. He was always restless, and his mind seemed to jump back and forth between thoughts. It wouldn't be until years later that people learned that his problems at school were due to an attention deficit disorder. People who have this learning disorder have short attention spans, so that it is difficult for them to concentrate. In Dan's early years, the problem went undiagnosed.

For a long time the O'Briens knew only that Dan was very hyperactive—that he couldn't sit still for more than a few minutes at a time. One way for Dan to expend his high level of energy, however, was through sports. He didn't have to sit still for very long when he was playing football, baseball, or basketball or running track. He grew into a tall and muscular youngster who could do well at everything athletic.

By the time he reached Henley High School in Klamath Falls in 1980, Dan was on the verge of becoming a star athlete. He was outstanding in football and basketball and even better at the running and jumping events in track and field.

Everything came easily to Dan in high school. He didn't have to work extra hard at sports to be a star.

His natural ability carried him through. And although his grades weren't great, he found that he could get by in school with little effort. He had more than enough natural intelligence, but he was simply too restless and had too short an attention span to concentrate in the classroom for very long.

In his senior year (1983–1984), Dan triumphed as an athlete. That fall he became an All-State performer with the Henley High football team. During the winter months, he achieved the same feat in basketball. When spring and the track season arrived, Dan O'Brien really had a chance to show off his stuff.

He was virtually unbeatable in the dashes, hurdles, and long jump. And when it came time for the Oregon state high school meet, he put on a spectacular one-man show.

Dan returns to visit Henley High School and his former track coach.

First he won the 100-meter dash. Next he finished first in the 110-meter high hurdles, which at the high school level are 39 inches off the ground. After that he was the winner in the 400-meter intermediate hurdles, which are 36 inches off the ground. And he finished the meet by winning his fourth state title in the long jump.

He had scored 40 points for Henley High all by himself. Only one complete team scored more. So as an individual, Dan finished second among all the teams entered. It was an amazing performance.

Having already reached his full height of 6 feet 2 inches and weighing 180 pounds, Dan had an almost perfect build for an all-around track star. He was slim enough for speed and jumping and big and strong enough for vaulting and throwing. So it was really no surprise when he decided to try the decathlon.

Shortly after the state championships, he entered the USA Junior Decathlon Championships. He had very little knowledge of the throwing events—the shot put, discus, and javelin—or the pole vault. But he was great in the running and jumping events, and he used his great athletic talent to get by in the others. He finished a surprising fourth in the competition, behind three other athletes who had already trained for all ten events.

Dan wanted to attend college. His first choice was the University of Oregon, where he hoped to compete in both football and track. But he needed a scholarship because his family couldn't afford to send him. Oregon made no offer, nor did several other schools to which he applied. Suddenly his options were very limited.

The only college coach who showed any real interest in Dan was Mike Keller, the track coach at the University of Idaho. Finally Dan accepted a full scholarship to Idaho, where he would begin studying and training to become a full-fledged national track star.

University of Idaho track coach Mike Keller recognized Dan's athletic talents when Dan was in high school and remained beside Dan throughout his career. Here he comforts Dan after Dan failed to make the 1992 Olympic team.

Chapter 3

A Real Goal

In the fall of 1984, Dan left Klamath Falls for the first time and arrived at the University of Idaho campus in Moscow, Idaho. Coach Keller hoped to develop Dan into a top performer in the decathlon. What the coach didn't expect was a young man who had never been away from home before and who simply wasn't ready for college.

"It was a mistake," Dan said later. "I should have gone to a junior college first. I wasn't a go-getter and couldn't get things done on my own. I didn't have a clue. I wasn't ready for college. I never studied."

Dan freely admits now that he wasn't mature enough to handle the responsibilities of college. By the time track season rolled around that spring, Dan's grades weren't good enough for him to join the team.

"Dan doesn't have a mean bone in his body," said Mike Keller. "But back then, he had no sense of responsibility. In 17 years of college coaching, I had just two athletes who weren't eligible to compete their first year. Dan was one of them."

He was away from home for the first time. It was easy to get hooked into a busy social life.

"I wanted to be a social giant," he admitted. "I wanted to party and have fun. High school was easy. You just go to class and get by. In college, it's not good enough to just go to class. You've got to study, and . . . take notes. My academic skills were just very weak, and I didn't take it seriously."

Dan's grades his first semester were two C's, a D, and an F. And they simply didn't get better. Twice more he was ineligible to compete—in his sophomore year (1986) and then in his junior year (1987). He was basically out of control. Fortunately his coach never gave up on him. He kept trying to find a way to encourage Dan to straighten out his life.

"Dan drove us crazy," said Mike Keller. "We spent most of our time dealing with Dan the person, not Dan the athlete."

It wasn't surprising that Dan finally lost his scholarship in 1986. The next year he moved into another student residence, or dorm, hoping to receive a student loan. It didn't come through. Nevertheless, he stayed in the dorm illegally, ate in the cafeteria, and continued to party. Finally Dan was informed that he owed the college $5,000, and the campus police removed him and all his belongings from the dorm.

Like most people in his situation, Dan reached an even lower point. It happened during winter break in

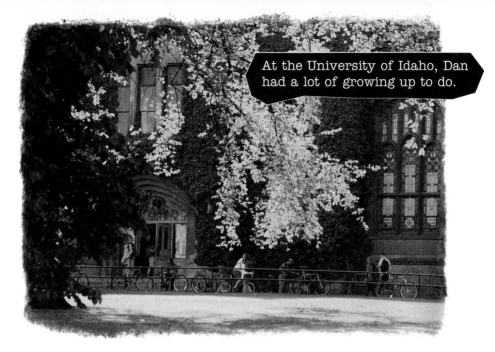

At the University of Idaho, Dan had a lot of growing up to do.

1987. He was out of school by then, had no money, and had stopped training completely.

"I was so disgusted with my life that I couldn't even face my family. Everyone at school had gone home. I stayed behind, hung out. . . . I was so depressed that the only way out I could see was to start training again. But I needed help, so I called a good friend. He gave me a second chance. Actually, I think it was about a fifth or sixth chance by then. But this time it changed my life."

That good friend was Mike Keller, the coach who had stuck by Dan since he had come to Idaho. Keller told Dan that the first thing he had to do was get back into school. He arranged for Dan to attend Spokane Community College, a junior college about 60 miles from the university. The coach also helped Dan pay his tuition for the spring semester of 1988.

"Basically, I kept him alive," the coach said. "I had to. There was no way I could let him die. If I hadn't helped him out, he'd be pushing a broom somewhere. Any coach would have done the same thing."

That wasn't entirely true. Mike Keller was exceptional in that he never lost faith in Dan O'Brien. He saw a great talent hidden somewhere inside the young man, if only Dan could put his life in order.

Dan worked hard, both in the classroom and on the track, during the spring of 1988. He did well enough to be readmitted to the University of Idaho for the 1988 fall semester. That summer Dan stayed in Moscow, Idaho, still working hard and training.

He had a job hauling bottled water and rock salt all over town. Dan recalled, "I'd get up at 5 in the morning to train, then work until 11 A.M., train again, and go back to work. I hated it."

The hard work soon paid off. Dan completed his first impressive decathlon, scoring 7,891 points. In the decathlon, a score of 8,300 or better is considered world-class. That meant that Dan was performing at nearly the same level of competition as the world's best decathletes. His score was good enough to qualify him for the 1988 Olympic Trials in Indianapolis, Indiana. In the trials, the best athletes in each event compete against each other for the honor of representing the United States in the Olympics.

Dan didn't do well in Indianapolis. He won the first event, the 100-meter dash. But in the long jump, he pulled a muscle at the back of his knee, so he had to withdraw from the rest of the competition.

Despite the injury, Dan saw the trials as a turning point. "As I was leaving the track in Indianapolis, I could see what the other guys were like," Dan recalled. "I realized they weren't better athletes than I was. They had more experience and knew the events better. That's all. Right then, I committed to doing better in school and applying myself on the track."

In the spring of 1989, Dan finally had the chance to compete for Mike Keller at Idaho. By the end of the season, he was favored to win the National Collegiate Athletic Association (NCAA) decathlon title. He had already scored a personal best of 7,987 points, but once again a knee injury kept him from competing, so he missed the NCAA championships.

Yet Dan was leaving Idaho in much better shape, both physically and emotionally, than could have been predicted less than two years earlier. He had left his partying days behind and found a real goal in his life. Although he had a long way to go, Dan was already thinking very big.

"It's easy to say now," he explained, "but even then I had a vision. It was the world record. I told my roommate I could break it. I guess I really had no business thinking that. Everything [all ten events of the decathlon] could be better, but I could see that if I put the practice time in, I could be really good." Finally Dan O'Brien was ready to go all out.

Chapter 4

A World-Class
Decathlete

Track-and-field events have never been very popular with the American public. Once in a while, but not often, a great track athlete comes along to catch the nation's fancy. The biggest world stage for track and field is the Olympic Games. And that occurs just once every four years.

When the legendary Jim Thorpe won the Olympic decathlon in Stockholm, Sweden, in 1912, King Gustav V of Sweden said to the young American, "Sir, you are the greatest athlete in the world."

Since that time the gold-medal winner of the Olympic decathlon has been known as the "world's greatest athlete." That is because so many different athletic skills are needed to complete all ten events. The ten events of the decathlon are as follows, in the order that they are run: 100-meter dash, long jump, shot put, high jump, 400-meter run, 110-meter high hurdles, discus throw, pole vault, javelin throw, and 1,500-meter run.

The first five events occur on the first day of competition. The other five events are held the next day.

A world-class decathlete must have a combination of great speed, great strength, and great endurance. He must also master the techniques of the seven events that involve more than just running.

The 100-meter dash is pure speed. A lightning start out of the starting blocks is very important. In the long jump, the athlete must run at great speed down the runway, take off at just the right spot, and then leap as far as he can. The "shot" used in the shot put is a 16-pound ball of iron. The athlete must be able to spin quickly in a small circle, then push the shot out from his shoulder as far as he can.

In the high jump, the athlete must have enough spring in his legs and the necessary technique to leap over a bar that is almost seven feet off the ground. The 400-meter run requires a combination of speed and endurance.

To do well in the 110-meter high hurdles, the athlete needs a good start and blazing speed. But he must also measure his steps between the hurdles, which are 42 inches high, and jump all ten of them cleanly, without losing speed. The discus is a round dish, thicker in the middle, that weighs 4 pounds 6.55 ounces. The athlete must spin quickly in a circle, then sail the disc as far as he can, with his arm snapping it out in an upward motion.

The pole vault is very difficult. The athlete must carry a long fiberglass pole as he runs toward the raised bar. Just before reaching the bar, he plants the pole in a three-sided box in the ground. He must use his strength to vault into the air, helped by the spring in the pole. He then flips his feet into the air and pushes off as the pole straightens, propelling his body over the bar.

The javelin is a light spear that cannot weigh less than 1 pound 12.25 ounces. It must be between 8 feet 6¼ inches and 8 feet 10¼ inches long. The athlete runs toward the release point and then throws the javelin like a baseball. Again, both speed and arm strength are important.

The final event is the 1,500-meter run, which takes a great deal of strength and endurance. So you can see how many skills a decathlete must master. He cannot simply practice one event like most other track athletes. He must practice ten events.

Besides having the kind of body that a decathlete needs, Dan is handsome, friendly, soft-spoken, and very honest, with the personality to be a very popular athlete with the public. He continued to work hard and improve. In early 1990 he was one of 16 talented athletes who went to San Francisco, California, to learn more about the decathlon. One of the instructors was Milt Campbell, who had won the decathlon gold medal in the 1956 Olympics.

In addition to teaching college athletes about the decathlon, Campbell made a suggestion. "Write down your goals," he told them. "Put them in your pocket, and look at them every day."

Here Dan chats with youth ambassadors from the Speedo Inner-City Games in Atlanta in July 1996. The Inner-City Games are athletic and academic competitions. Their purpose is to offer children a positive alternative to drugs and violence.

Dan found a piece of paper and wrote that he wanted to be the world's greatest athlete. He carried that paper with him everywhere after that.

That summer Dan participated in his first international meet—the 1990 Goodwill Games in Seattle, Washington. After the first five events, he had a 300-point lead over United States National Champion Dave Johnson. Dan was in a strong position to win. Though weaker in the second day's events, he still held a small lead going into the final event, the 1,500-meter run.

The 1,500 was Dan's worst event, and Johnson beat him by some ten seconds, winning enough points to overcome Dan's lead. Despite his second-place finish,

Dan had proved that he was not only a world-class performer but close to being the world's best. Still, Coach Keller saw several things during the Goodwill Games that proved Dan needed more work.

"The 1,500 showed that Dan doesn't have very good competitive instincts yet," the coach said. "He also has to learn to focus on his own performance, not someone else's." In other words Dan had to stop worrying about how the other decathletes were performing. His coach also felt that for Dan to continue to improve, he would need some special coaching.

"I could see the enormity of what Dan could accomplish," the coach said. "He needed more coaching in the throwing and jumping events. That was beyond me. Rick Sloan was the best field event man in the country, and he was willing to help."

Sloan was the track coach at nearby Washington State University and had finished seventh in the decathlon at the 1968 Olympics. He, too, thought Dan had tremendous potential but also some flaws.

"Dan doesn't have an aggressive personality," Sloan said. "He's simply not tough enough. It's a mental thing with him. He's not willing to push through the pain or do whatever it takes to win."

Dan was living in Moscow by then, so he could still train with Mike Keller at Idaho. He was also close enough to Washington State to train with Rick Sloan. He began working out three times a day, a total of eight hours, six days a week. It was a very vigorous schedule.

In the morning he ran a lot, sometimes doing intervals, which means he alternated speed work and slower runs. At other times he took long, easy runs. After lunch Dan drove to Washington State, where he practiced the shot put, javelin, discus, jumps, and vaults under the watchful eye of Coach Sloan. Next he returned to Idaho for a late-day workout. He then either ran some more or worked on his hurdles, before finishing with lifting weights.

It was a difficult schedule, and Dan was the first to admit that training wasn't always easy. "Doing a decathlon is definitely fun," Dan observed, "but the training isn't. The thing I love about the decathlon is, you always get another chance. Plus you get to do ten different things. But training is more of a job. What motivates me is feeling good about myself. I love that bouncy feeling when everything is going great. Sometimes I feel so good, so right that I'm getting it. Other times, nothing works. It's hard to work on the weakest events because they feel the weirdest."

Dan went on to explain how the 1,500 felt, when he ran it as the tenth and last event of a two-day grind. "I'm afraid of it," he said. "The pain scares me. I think I'm going to die. My legs are shaking, and I have that achy, queasy feeling. My stomach's churning, and I've got the cold sweats because I'm so nervous."

But Dan kept working, and soon it began paying off. All that training, combined with his natural ability, was showing big results. In the 1991 United

States Championship, he not only won the decathlon but scored an incredible 8,844 points, just 3 points shy of Daley Thompson's world record.

Dan then went to the World Championship in Tokyo, Japan, where he again dominated his event. Again he was close to breaking the world record. If he had run a faster 1,500 meters, he could have done it. But Dan still won the gold medal with 8,812 points.

Barcelona, Spain, was where the 1992 Olympic Games would be held. Dan was now the overwhelming favorite to win Olympic gold. Nearly everyone in the world of track and field thought that he would do it. Daley Thompson, the British world-record holder and two-time Olympic champion, already thought that Dan was a better decathlete than he was.

"He's bigger, stronger, and faster than I am," said Thompson. The stage was set for Dan to let the whole world know how good he had become.

Dan throws the javelin during the 1991 World Championship in Tokyo. Dan won a gold medal.

Chapter 5

A Crushing Defeat

There was a time when only amateur athletes could go to the Olympics. Amateur athletes are athletes who have not turned professional. Only professionals receive money for competing in a sport. Amateur athletes, then, have to find a way to support themselves while training. When Bruce Jenner trained for the decathlon for the 1976 Olympics, his wife supported him financially by working as a flight attendant. But since then the rules have changed. Both professional and amateur athletes can now compete in the Olympics.

By the time he began preparing for the 1992 Olympic Trials, Dan had signed advertising contracts with such companies as Visa, Fuji Film, Reebok, Texaco, Ray Ban, and the Idaho State Potato Commission. So he was already earning a good deal of money. That was one less worry for an athlete who trained eight hours a day, six days a week.

Yet Dan also followed a simple lifestyle, living with a friend in a two-bedroom apartment near the Idaho campus. He owned few material possessions.

Here's Dan at right with Dave Johnson, his friend and decathlon competitor.

His apartment had a television and a quality stereo system. But he usually rode to and from the track on a bike, and he didn't own a car.

Dan continued to be the gold-medal favorite. Many thought that his toughest competition would come from a fellow American, Dave Johnson. On Super Bowl Sunday, in late January of 1992, Reebok began a series of television and print ads featuring the two decathlon stars. Dubbed the "Dave & Dan campaign," the ads showed both athletes training for the various events, with the gold medal as their goal. The end of each ad had the tag line: "To be settled in Barcelona."

That meant that Dan O'Brien and Dave Johnson would finish their rivalry at the Olympics, with one or the other on the winner's stand, receiving the gold medal. Both of them, of course, wore Reebok shoes in the ads. The company was said to have spent between $25 million and $30 million on the campaign.

Finally it was the last week in June, the time for the trials. America's finest track-and-field stars gathered in New Orleans, Louisiana. What many people didn't know was that Dan wasn't completely healthy. Already called the most talented decathlete who ever lived, Dan was recovering from a stress fracture of his right shinbone, just below the knee. The injury had happened in February, and for a month Dan could run only in a swimming pool, where the water's resistance made movement easy.

He and his coaches felt that the injury was nearly 100 percent healed. But there was one event that worried him—the pole vault. Because of the injury, Dan had not vaulted in a single meet all spring.

Yet during the first day of competition, Dan looked great. He did well in all five events: the 100, the 400, the high jump, the long jump, and the shot put, in which he had achieved a personal best of 54 feet 5½ inches. His 4,698 points not only placed him well in the lead but set a world record for the first day's competition.

Dan tosses the shot at the 1992 Olympic Trials.

Dan began the second day by scoring well in the 110-meter hurdles and the discus throw. Leading Dave Johnson by an astounding total of 512 points, he was on the way to setting a world record. Now it was time for the pole vault. Dan's personal best in the vault was 17 feet ¾ inch. If he even came close to that, the world record would be almost a sure bet.

Because he didn't want to put too much strain on his left leg, Dan chose not to attempt to vault on four early heights. If he had cleared any one of them, he would have received points. Instead Dan decided to take his first vault when the bar was set at 15 feet 9 inches.

On his first try, he lost control of the pole and somersaulted below the bar. His coaches began to worry. If Dan didn't clear the bar in one of his two last tries, he wouldn't score any points. And if that happened, there was no way that he could finish in the top three and go on to the Olympics.

Then came his second try. Dan ran down the runway, planted the pole, and got up high enough. But instead of pushing his body over the bar, he came down on top of it. He had missed twice. He had just one more try. If he

Dan puts his head down after failing to qualify for the 1992 Olympic decathlon team.

missed again, he would "no-height," or not score any points.

Twice Dan started down the runway and stopped. He didn't feel that his steps were right. On his third and final try, he was out of sync, or out of step, once again.

Dan watches from the sidelines during the 1992 Olympics, for which he failed to qualify to be on the U.S. team.

Dan planted the pole and began to swing up. But he saw that he wasn't going to make it. He simply curled his body and fell back to the ground. The entire stadium was shocked into silence.

The world's best decathlete, as many had called him, would not go to the Olympics. Only the top three finishers make the team. Dan completed the last two events. But because he had scored no points in the pole vault, he was in 11th place when the competition ended. A successful pole vault of just 9 feet 2 inches would have earned him enough points to make the team.

"I felt numb at first," Dan said later. "I wanted to turn to somebody and say, 'Hey, this shouldn't be happening to me.'"

But it had happened. Dan and his coaches had felt that a vault of 15 feet 9 inches was a safe place to start.

Even Dan's main competitor, Dave Johnson, was unhappy with the results. "I don't know how good our system is," Johnson said, "if it doesn't get Dan O'Brien to the Olympics."

Chapter 6

A World Record and New Hope

To see Dan O'Brien not make the Olympic team was the biggest shock the track-and-field world had received in years. Even Dan said that it really didn't sink in until he flew home to Idaho after the trials. "That's when I realized it was over," he said.

Mike Keller compared Dan's failure to "a death in the family." His other coach, Rick Sloan, felt that it was important for Dan to start training again.

"That's when the real healing begins," Sloan said. "When you take that first step toward your next goal."

To Dan's credit, he didn't run and hide. He still made some TV appearances with Dave Johnson and then went to the Olympics as a television commentator. He watched Johnson struggle with an injured ankle and win a bronze medal for finishing third. Dan still wished more than anything that he could have competed. Yet Rick Sloan spoke for many others when he said, "The way Dan handled not making the team endeared him to people around the world."

Dan soon set another goal. "I know I can break the world record," he said.

A month after the Olympics, Dan entered a meet in Stockholm, Sweden. As usual he was the favorite to win. But this time he failed to clear his opening height in the high jump. He received no points again. He didn't finish the competition, and people began to wonder if his failure in the Olympic Trials had left a lasting mark.

In September 1992 Dan traveled to the town of Talence, France, for a special kind of track meet. There were only two events: the decathlon and the heptathlon, which consists of seven track-and-field events. All the best decathletes in the world were there, including Olympic champion Robert Zmelik, of the Czech Republic.

Dan opened the competition by running the 100-meter dash in 10.43 seconds, earning a 75-point lead over Zmelik after just one event. After the dash Zmelik's coach turned to Mike Keller and said, "We both know that if Dan had been at the Olympics, it would have been a different story."

Dan continued to shine. In the long jump, he sailed 26 feet 6¼ inches. That was the longest non-wind-aided long jump ever achieved in a decathlon. In the shot put, he tossed a personal best of 54 feet 9¼ inches. His high jump and 400-meter dash were good for him, but they were not exceptional. Yet after the first day and five events, he had 4,720 points. He was far ahead of Zmelik and 43 points ahead of Daley Thompson's world record.

After his failure at the 1992 Olympic Trials, Dan roared back. In September at the decathlon competition in Talence, France, he emerged with a new world decathlon record. Here he is making the longest non-wind-aided long jump ever in a decathlon.

On the second day, every seat was filled at the stadium, and every fan was urging Dan to break the record. He started the second day by running the

110-meter hurdles in 13.98 seconds, just 0.04 seconds off (slower than) his personal best. Next he threw the discus 159 feet 2 inches for yet another personal best. He was still on record-setting pace with the third event, the dreaded pole vault.

The winds were swirling around the stadium, making it a bit harder than usual. Dan decided to start vaulting at 15 feet 1 inch, with the bar 8 inches lower than the height he had failed to clear at the Olympic Trials.

Yet on his first attempt, Dan didn't come close to clearing the bar. Would his bad fortune continue? Then, on his second try, he put it all together and sailed over with room to spare. He went on to clear 16 feet 4¾ inches, a good vault for him. The points continued to pile up.

"I boomed that one," he said, of his first clear vault. "It was big."

Next came the javelin, and Dan exploded for a new personal best of 205 feet 4 inches. Now only the tiring 1,500-meter run remained. Dan was told that he had to run it in just 4 minutes 49 seconds to break the world record. That was 16 seconds slower than his personal best. But he hated the 1,500, and he still needed to make a big effort to make 4:49.

Dan ran around the track with dogged determination, trying to coax every ounce of strength out of his tired body. As he came around the final turn, the crowd was screaming, urging him on.

Dan breaks his unlucky streak and sails over the bar in the pole vault at Talence in September 1992.

"The last 100 meters, I could see the clock," he said. "I knew I was going to make it."

Dan crossed the finish line in 4:42.10 (4 minutes 42 seconds 10 hundredths of a second). He had done it! His final point total was 8,891, a new world record. And he had beaten the second-place finisher, Olympic champ Zmelik, by an amazing 547 points. That's how powerful his performance had been.

Afterward a happy Dan O'Brien declared, "The world's greatest athlete has come back to America."

What he meant was that no American had held the decathlon world record since Bruce Jenner in 1976. Now Dan had reclaimed it for his country. But there was still one more thing to prove—one more barrier to overcome.

Chapter 7

Olympic Gold at Last

After breaking the world record, Dan continued to set goals. He said that he wanted to hit the 9,000-point mark. But he would have to wait almost four years before realizing his biggest goal—to capture that Olympic gold medal.

"If I don't [win the gold medal], my career won't be complete," he said. "As I get closer to Atlanta [the site of the 1996 Olympic Games], everybody's going to start focusing on the pole vault. It's something you never forget. Every decathlon, in my first attempt in the pole vault, I always think about what happened in '92. It's my motivation not to make a mistake like that again."

Dan continued to win. By most outward appearances, he was still the best decathlete in the world. But there were times when his fears and self-doubts would surface. Before the United States National Championship in 1993 (an event that he won), his coaches literally had to push him onto the track to begin the first event. "He had a look of absolute terror in his eyes," said Fred Samara, decathlon coach of the United States team.

Still, a year later, at the 1994 USA/Mobil Track & Field Championship, held in June in Knoxville, Tennessee, Dan was brilliant. At the end of nine events, he was close to another world record. He needed a time of 4:43.97 in the 1,500 to break his own record. Yet he went on and jogged through in 5:16.42. He still won the title by 159 points, but he didn't break the record.

"Sure, I'm disappointed," he said. "I let this one slide a bit."

It was at about this time that longtime coach Mike Keller began to understand something about Dan that had always puzzled him. The coach's 16-year-old son, Travis, had recently been diagnosed with attention deficit hyperactivity disorder (ADHD). Coach Keller wanted to know more about the problem.

"I was reading a book about it," the coach recalled. "On every page I found myself writing 'Dan–Travis' and 'Travis–Dan' in the margin."

The coach's son and the world's best decathlete showed many of the same behavioral patterns. For example, like Travis, Dan had trouble concentrating, even for short periods of time. Coach Keller wondered if Dan suffered from ADHD. He suggested that Dan see Jim Reardon, a former discus thrower and now a counseling psychologist. After running tests on Dan, Reardon said that there was a good chance that Dan had ADHD. Dan then saw a doctor, who prescribed a medication used to treat ADHD.

After taking it for a while, Dan said, "I can think more clearly." He said that he was also more focused and more confident. Coach Keller agreed. "We've seen a big change in him," he said.

However, that wasn't the end of the problem. It was determined later that the medication was giving Dan severe headaches and leaving him unable to sleep. He had to stop taking it. Now he had to use willpower alone to overcome his ADHD.

"The diagnosis was the main thing, because it explained a lot of things," Dan said about his ADHD. "It's made me understand this is why I was a bad student, this is why I couldn't concentrate, this is why I had trouble reading. But it's by no means an excuse for not getting good grades or not being able to concentrate."

Dan began to use deep-breathing techniques to help him concentrate and focus. Now that he was finally aware of his problem, he could work to overcome it.

Dr. Frank Zarnowski, a decathlon historian, was amazed by the way Dan handled his problems. "Dan O'Brien is a great story," he said. "He's a role model. Here is a guy who's had some problems, overcame them, and has been big enough to say, 'Yeah, I've made mistakes.' How many people can do that? And he's still the best in the world.

"When I watch him now, he's the most focused guy out there. Remember, the decathlon is not like a single event. This is two days of focusing and concentrating. What he's done is amazing."

Psychologist Jim Reardon continued to work with Dan. Reardon said that what had happened in the 1992 Olympic Trials had been a real trauma for Dan.

"What Dan experienced in 1992 would clearly qualify as trauma, because it was so unexpected. For trauma victims, anniversaries are always difficult. They trigger fear and anxiety."

So with the 1996 Olympic Trials approaching, the people around Dan began to worry, even though he had won every major event for the last four years, including his third World Championship in 1995.

"The moment of highest tension at the trials will come when Dan gets on the runway for the [pole] vault," Reardon predicted. "Everyone will stop, every camera in the stadium will focus on him, and everyone will wonder: Will he get over?"

Dan didn't hide. He spent a great deal of time talking to kids at schools and within his own Dan O'Brien Youth Foundation, which holds meets for youngsters. The foundation sponsors a National High School Decathlon Championship, held yearly in his hometown of Klamath Falls. The most talented young decathletes in the country gather for the event, which encourages youngsters to learn all the events of the decathlon and begin competing.

Dan also was always ready to discuss his own problems and what he had to do to overcome them.

Here Dan warms up in May 1996 with California children from the Participation in the Lives of America's Youth (P.L.A.Y.) program. The program encourages children to become involved in positive activities like sports.

"I'm not trying to be a role model," Dan has said. "But I like to show kids that it's cool to get your work done instead of goofing off and being a jerk. So I visit classrooms or walk over to the local school and have lunch with kids. I like to show them there's hope. Look at me. I wasn't a great athlete until I started to work hard."

The 1996 Olympic Trials were held in the brand new Olympic Stadium in Atlanta, Georgia. It was the same stadium in which the Olympics would be held nearly two months later. So all the American athletes would be on their home turf.

Dan, of course, was the favorite in the decathlon. Although pushed by the up-and-coming Chris Huffins during the first day's competition, Dan began pulling away during the opening events of day two.

Then came the pole vault. As Dan got set for his first try at 14 feet 9 inches, the stadium fell silent. Everyone remembered what had happened in the 1992 trials when he had no-heighted the pole vault. In the vast quiet, Dan got set, sprinted down the runway, planted the pole—and soared over the bar! The people in the stadium erupted with cheering. There would be no repeat of 1992.

Dan finally cleared 17 feet ¾ inch in the vault. He was so pumped up that in the next event, he threw the javelin a personal best of 214 feet. He won the competition and then prepared to achieve his final goal: the Olympic gold medal.

Dan (second from left) clears the first hurdle in the men's decathlon 110-meter hurdles during the 1996 Olympics.

The Olympic event wasn't an easy decathlon for Dan. He wasn't worried anymore about what had happened in the pole vault in 1992. Instead, it was strong competition from Germany's Frank Busemann that made Dan work hard for his expected victory.

After the first day, Dan led Busemann by just 124 points. Because the first five events were always Dan's strong performances, some people worried that Busemann could overtake him.

Surprisingly, the turning point in the competition was the pole vault. Dan cleared his opening height easily and went on to vault 16 feet 4¾ inches. He scored 910 points in the event, increasing his lead over Busemann.

Energized by his success in the pole vault, Dan threw the javelin 219 feet 6 inches, a personal best. He just had to hang on in the 1,500-meter run.

On his way to Olympic gold, Dan throws the discus during the 1996 games.

And that's just what Dan did. Encouraged by the chants of "U–S–A," "U–S–A," "U–S–A," he stayed close enough to Busemann to win the gold medal by just 18 points. Even though the margin of victory was narrow, Dan's 8,824 points set an Olympic record.

"I've thought about this every single day for the last four years," Dan said, after winning the gold. "You can't describe it. It's an amazing feeling. . . . I was running the 1,500 and thinking that I'm tired, I'm numb, it hurts. But it's supposed to feel that way."

Dan plans to continue competing. But he may not compete long enough for another Olympics. It depends on how his 30-plus-year-old body holds up.

There are financial rewards that go with being called the world's greatest athlete. Dan's contracts

Dan and other U.S. decathlete gold medalists show off jackets with their names and the year of their medals on them.

Dan has become world famous since he won his Olympic gold. Here he is with another famous 1996 gold medalist, track star Michael Johnson.

to represent various companies total more than $600,000 a year. Winning Olympic gold will lead to more opportunities for the well-spoken O'Brien.

But Dan deserves his success. He had to overcome many obstacles on his road to the Olympic gold medal. He had to learn the value of hard work. He had to set goals and forget about having fun all the time. He had to overcome an attention deficit disorder. And finally, he had to overcome the trauma of failing to make the 1992 Olympic team and the obstacle of failing at the pole vault.

"I don't know what's going to happen from here on out," he said. "But I feel like [winning the gold medal] is a new place to start some things in my life. I don't think I've competed to my full potential yet."

U.S. Olympic
Decathlon Winners

Year	Gold Medal Winner	Location	Point Total
1912	Jim Thorpe	Stockholm, Sweden	6,564
1924	Harold Osborn	Paris, France	6,476
1932	James Bausch	Los Angeles, California	6,735
1936	Glenn Morris	Berlin, Germany	7,254
1948	Bob Mathias	London, England	6,628
1952	Bob Mathias	Helsinki, Finland	7,580
1956	Milt Campbell	Melbourne, Australia	7,565
1960	Rafer Johnson	Rome, Italy	7,901
1968	Bill Toomey	Mexico City, Mexico	8,158
1976	Bruce Jenner	Montreal, Canada	8,634
1996	Dan O'Brien	Atlanta, Georgia	8,824

Note: Early point totals are revised to conform to current standards.

Major Championships
Won by Dan O'Brien

Year	Event	Location	Point Total
1991	U.S. Championship	New York, New York	8,844
1991	World Championship	Tokyo, Japan	8,812
1993	U.S. Championship	Eugene, Oregon	8,331
1993	World Championship	Stuttgart, Germany	8,817
1994	U.S. Championship	Knoxville, Tennessee	8,707
1995	U.S. Championship	Sacramento, California	8,682
1995	World Championship	Gothenburg, Sweden	8,695
1996	U.S. Olympic Trials	Atlanta, Georgia	8,726
1996	26th Olympic Games	Atlanta, Georgia	8,824

Dan O'Brien's Personal Bests and Point Totals

Event	Best Time or Distance	Point Value
100-meter dash	10.36 seconds	1,008
Long jump	26 feet 6¼ inches	1,081
Shot put	54 feet 9½ inches	894
High jump	7 feet 2½ inches	992
400-meter run	46.53 seconds	982
110-meter high hurdles	13.47 seconds	1,043
Discus throw	173 feet 5 inches	930
Pole vault	17 feet 2¾ inches	988
Javelin throw	219 feet 6 inches	842
1,500-meter run	4 minutes 33.19 seconds	724

Note: If all of Dan's personal bests had been in the same meet, his point total would be 9,484 points.

The Fight for the Decathlon World Record Since 1976

Record Holder and Country	Date Set	Point Total
Bruce Jenner, United States	July 30, 1976	8,634
Daley Thompson, Great Britain	May 18, 1980	8,648
Guido Kratschmer, Germany	June 15, 1980	8,667
Daley Thompson, Great Britain	May 23, 1982	8,730
Jurgen Hingsen, Germany	August 15, 1982	8,741
Daley Thompson, Great Britain	September 8, 1982	8,774
Jurgen Hingsen, Germany	June 5, 1983	8,825
Jurgen Hingsen, Germany	June 9, 1984	8,832
Daley Thompson, Great Britain	August 9, 1984	8,847
Dan O'Brien, United States	September 5, 1992	8,891

Further Reading

Arnold, Caroline. *The Olympic Summer Games.* New York: Watts, 1991.

Assen, Nathan. *Bruce Jenner.* Minneapolis: Lerner, 1979.

Cohen, Neil. *Jackie Joyner-Kersee.* Boston: Little, Brown, 1992.

Emert, Phyllis Raybin. *Illustrated Track and Field Dictionary for Young People.* New York: Harvey House, 1981.

Goldstein, Margaret. *Jackie Joyner-Kersee.* Minneapolis: Lerner, 1994.

McMane, Fred. *Track & Field Basics.* Englewood Cliffs, NJ: Prentice-Hall, 1992.

Rosenthal, Bert. *Track and Field.* Austin, TX: Raintree Steck-Vaughn, 1994.

Index